# USING BIRTH, MARRIAGE
## *and* DEATH RECORDS

*Public Record Office*
**Pocket Guides to Family History**

Getting Started in Family History

Using Birth, Marriage and Death Records

Using Census Returns

Using Wills

Using Army Records

Using Navy Records

# USING BIRTH, MARRIAGE

## *and* DEATH RECORDS

PUBLIC RECORD OFFICE

Public Record Office
Richmond
Surrey
TW9 4DU

ISBN 1 873162 88 X

A catalogue card for this book
is available from the British Library

Front cover: wedding party of Mr Burnell, taken near
Westersham, Kent, on 7 May 1892  (PRO COPY 1/408)

Printed by Cromwell Press Ltd, Trowbridge, Wilts.

# CONTENTS

# INTRODUCTION

More and more people are wanting to research the history and experiences of their own family. There has been an explosion of interest in this most democratic form of historical research, and family historians are now amongst the keenest users of Britain's unrivalled archives. As a family historian, you will need to look in all kinds of records kept by local or central government, by the church or state, or even by your own forebears. About the only things these records will have in common is that they were not written with you or your questions in mind – and that they are all likely to raise further questions!

Births, marriages and deaths are the events that give us the outline of our ancestors' lives. As you start discovering the broad outline of your family tree, don't get fixated on going back as far as you can, as fast as you can. As you discover new ancestors, try to find out more about them – a bare tree can't compare to one in leaf. Your family's experience of life, as you uncover it, will provide you with a unique perspective on history. We hope that this Pocket Guide together with the others in the series will act as companions on your journey into the past.

# GETTING STARTED

When you want to find out about your family history, the best way to start is with your own history. Make a list of all the dates and all the relatives you can remember. Ask as many of your relations as possible to do the same, and listen again to the family's favourite (and less well known) reminiscences to see what clues they provide. Question your elderly relatives closely – but tactfully! Much of what they say will give you details of peoples' lives and personalities that you can never get from records.

When you have your lists, you may find that a good deal of checking can be done at home. Look through old papers and records, and ask everyone in your family to look in their attics for more evidence. Old photographs and treasured possessions are useful and evocative, but documents are invaluable. They provide the basis of your research, and will save a lot of time and some money. Unless you are unlucky you should soon be able to compile a checklist of likely dates and events in the lives of your recent ancestors. There will inevitably be some gaps in your list and some queries. From these you will be able to develop a line of enquiry and a plan for your initial research.

If you can discover the dates of births, marriages and deaths for as many people as possible in your family, you have the beginnings of a family tree. Now the real search begins – to find as much detail as you can, and to move back into the unremembered past.

# RESEARCH TECHNIQUES

## Check the basic facts

The checklist you have compiled by consulting your family is your starting point but, before you go any further, it is important to check your facts for accuracy. Memory is fallible, people may not be candid, and it can be very misleading to rely on the spoken word rather than the official record. Take, for instance, the case of the researcher who scoured the marriage records of 1923 for the exact date of her aunt's wedding only to find after hours of searching that the wedding took place the following year, shortly before the birth of the first baby. The aunt had hidden the truth so successfully that nobody else in the family knew about it. Something like this can lead you not only to the 'truth', but also to a greater understanding of the pressures she and her husband must have faced, not just at the time, but on every anniversary, to conceal what was then seen as a cause for real shame.

Checking the details of births, marriages and deaths in the recent past and for much of the 19th century is relatively easy because of the system of civil (state) registration that was set up in 1837. Your family may have kept the actual birth, marriage and death certificates of your parents, grandparents and other relatives. If not, you will probably want to obtain copies of at least some of them, from the registers kept by the various registry offices. Details of how to do this are given below: what you need to know now is that you do not have free access to the registers themselves, only to their indexes, and that you have to buy copies of any certificates you want to inspect.

These certificates (whether originals or purchased copies) will give you a wealth of detail about who your forebears were, where they lived, and perhaps even their occupations. They should also open up further potential lines of enquiry.

## Work methodically

First of all it is important to start with what you know to be fact and to work backwards methodically. If you know that your grandmother died in 1970 but are not sure when she was born, look in the indexes to the registers of deaths first. If you find her there, you will also find some useful information with which to search further, even without buying a copy of the death certificate itself. For instance, you will find her age of death so that you have firmer (but not proven) evidence on which to base your search of the birth indexes.

## Take notes

Keep a careful note of all the information you discover, even if you can't immediately see its usefulness. It may turn out to be of use later, and you will be unlikely to hold all the detail in your head. You may know your grandmother's first name, for instance, but not her second name. The death register might give you her second name or at least

## Tips for getting started

- Find as much information as possible at home first.

- Check your basic facts in the official records.

- Keep your notes in as well organised a way as you can manage, or you will get swamped with information.

- Don't place too much significance on small differences in surnames. Dropping your 'aitches' was as common in the written word as in the spoken word. The following letters were often interchanged: T with D; G with K; P with R.

- Work your way methodically back in time from the recent dates you know – trying to jump a long way back may set you off on the wrong track!

its initial. Knowing this initial may help you to find her name in the other registers when you look for more details of her life, and to distinguish her from other people with the same or similar names. As people were frequently given the names of godparents or members of the family, notes of all forenames can be very useful in providing clues!

## Check the alternatives

Do not assume that all the information given in the indexes is necessarily correct. It is easy for mistakes to occur. You might know that your family has always spelt its surname as 'Gardiner', but if you cannot find a record under this spelling it is worth trying 'Gardner' or 'Gardener'. Another common cause of confusion is when people have given an incorrect age at their wedding. The bride might have wished to appear younger than the groom, or at least younger than she was. Either the bride or the groom could have been younger than the age of consent.

# PLACES YOU MAY NEED TO VISIT OR CONTACT

## Your local library

Many library services now offer two things which will be of great value to you: access to the internet, and their own collections of material for family and local history. You may not find these at a branch library, but you should at the central library.

Access to the internet itself will bring many sources for family history much closer to hand. Some internet addresses have been given in this Pocket Guide – there are *very* many more websites on family history.

To find out what sources are available near you, you need to access a service on the internet called *Familia* (http://www.earl.org.uk/familia/). This is a directory of family history resources held in public libraries in the UK and Ireland. Each library has provided information on whether they hold any of the following:

• Registrar General's indexes to births, marriages and deaths from 1837 (England and Wales) or from 1855 (Scotland)
• parish registers 16th to 20th centuries
• *International Genealogical Index*
• census returns 1841–1891
• directories 18th to 20th centuries
• electoral registers and poll books 18th to 20th centuries
• unpublished indexes
• newspapers
• periodicals
• photographs

## Family Records Centre (FRC)

The Family Records Centre, in central London, is where indexes to the main collections of birth, marriage, death (since 1837) and census records (since 1841) can be consulted. It was set up by the Office for National Statistics (ONS) – the new parent department of the old General Register Office – and by the Public Record Office (PRO), to be a 'one-stop shop'. If you live within a reasonable distance of London, this is the place to start.

► Family Records Centre
1 Myddelton Street
London EC1R 1UW
General telephone: 020 8392 5300
Telephone for birth, marriage and death certificates:
0151 471 4800
Fax: 020 8392 5307
Internet: http://www.pro.gov.uk/
ONS website: http://www.ons.gov.uk/

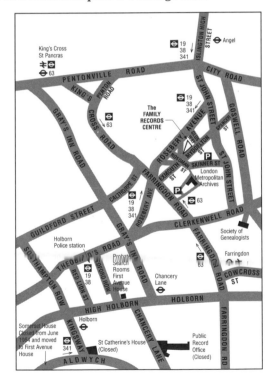

You can visit the FRC in person without an appointment (see also pp. 31–2).

Opening times (closed Sundays and Bank Holidays)

| Monday | 9 a.m. to 5 p.m. |
| Tuesday | 10 a.m. to 7 p.m. |
| Wednesday | 9 a.m. to 5 p.m. |
| Thursday | 9 a.m. to 7 p.m. |
| Friday | 9 a.m. to 5 p.m. |
| Saturday | 9.30 a.m. to 5 p.m. |

## Family History Centres of the Church of Jesus Christ of Latter-day Saints (LDS)

The LDS has a network of Family History Centres throughout the UK, where you can search a wide collection of microfilmed indexes and records. If coming to London is inconvenient, you will find these Centres a boon. You don't have to be a member of the Church. To find your local Centre, contact the Genealogical Society of Utah at the following address:

▶ Genealogical Society of Utah
  British Isles Family History Service Centre
  185 Penns Lane
  Sutton Coldfield
  West Midlands B76 8JU

# General or local Register Offices

These are where the records of births, marriages and deaths are actually kept, although you don't get direct access to them. The rules differ from place to place, and some run a postal or e-mail service only. You can contact them directly to buy a certificate: they can do a limited amount of index searching for a fee, plus the cost of the copy. For how to contact local offices, see pp. 29.

▼ General Register Office of England and Wales
(also known as Office for National Statistics)
PO Box 2
Southport
Merseyside PR8 2JD
Telephone: 0151 471 4800
Internet: http://www.ons.gov.uk/
For searching the indexes yourself, see pp. 14–16.

▼ General Register Office of Ireland
Joyce House
8–11 Lombard Street
Dublin 2
Telephone: 00353 1 6711863

▼ General Register Office (Northern Ireland) ·
Oxford House
Chichester Street
Belfast BT1 4HL
Telephone: 028 9025 2000
Internet: http://www.nisra.gov.uk/gro/

▼ General Register Office for Scotland
  New Register House
  3 West Register Street
  Edinburgh EH1 3YT
  Telephone: 0131 334 0380
  Fax: 0131 314 4400
  Internet: http://www.open.gov.uk/gros/groshome.htm

▼ Office for National Statistics
  See General Register Office of England and Wales above.

## Public Record Office (PRO) and local record offices

The Public Record Office is the United Kingdom's national archive, at Kew in Surrey. It is not the place to start, but it may be a place to look for some leaves for your tree!

Local record offices (usually for a county or a borough) have their own sets of local archives to provide more branches for your family tree – especially parish registers. Many have purchased copies of indexes or records on microfilm or microfiche from the General Register Office or the Public Record Office.

Most record offices don't have the staff to run a research service: you are expected to come and do the research yourself, among the records. Don't worry – they are well used to family historians, and try to make the whole experience as little daunting as possible. However, there is something about the volume of evidence from the past, and the first sight of a real old document, that tends to make anybody's first day at a record office slightly nerve-racking. Just remember that everyone there had a similar first day – including the staff!

Record offices are able to give advice, and many produce leaflets on the sources they hold. Have a look at the PRO website if you can, to get an idea of the range of finding aids and records available at Kew.

If you really can't get to a record office yourself, you can ask a friend to go for you, or you can employ an independent record agent. Many advertise in the family history magazines: there is also a list on the PRO website. It's a good idea to read the advice on employing an independent researcher on the website of the Society of Genealogists – http://www.sog.org.uk/

▼ Public Record Office
  Kew
  Richmond
  Surrey TW9 4DU
  General telephone: 020 8876 3444
  Telephone number for enquiries: 020 8392 5200
  Telephone number for advance ordering of documents (with exact references only): 020 8392 5260
  Internet: http://www.pro.gov.uk/

Opening times (closed Sundays and Bank Holidays)

| | |
|---|---|
| Monday | 9.00 a.m. to 5 p.m. |
| Tuesday | 10 a.m. to 7 p.m. |
| Wednesday | 9.00 a.m. to 5 p.m. |
| Thursday | 9.00 a.m. to 7 p.m. |
| Friday | 9.00 a.m. to 5 p.m. |
| Saturday | 9.30 a.m. to 5 p.m. |

## Society of Genealogists (SoG)

The Society of Genealogists, in London, is the premier family history society, with a wonderful library that is a major resource in its own right. You can become a member for a fee and an annual subscription, or you can use the library for a fee.

▼ Society of Genealogists
14 Charterhouse Buildings
Goswell Road
London EC1M 7BA
Telephone: 020 7251 8799
Internet: http://www.sog.org.uk/

Opening times (closed Sundays and Mondays)

| | |
|---|---|
| Tuesday | 10 a.m. to 6 p.m. |
| Wednesday | 10 a.m. to 8 p.m. |
| Thursday | 10 a.m. to 8 p.m. |
| Friday | 10 a.m. to 6 p.m. |
| Saturday | 10 a.m. to 6 p.m. |

## Federation of Family History Societies (FFHS)

Contact the Federation to find out about the large number of local family history societies. Among the members are people from all walks of life, who have turned their various skills and unvaried enthusiasm and energy into the hunt for their own family history, and to the task of making sources for family history known and available. Many index records of no direct interest to themselves, on the understanding that someone, somewhere else, is indexing just the set of records they always needed and never knew existed. Family historians in these societies seem to discover new friends at an even greater rate than 'new' ancestors!

▼ Federation of Family History Societies
Benson Room
Birmingham and Midland Institute
Margaret Street
Birmingham B3 3BS

# CIVIL REGISTRATION OF BIRTHS, MARRIAGES AND DEATHS IN THE UK

Civil registration is the state's legally recognised system of recording the birth, marriage(s) and death of people resident in Britain. The copy certificates that you can purchase are legal documents that prove the registration. Make sure you don't get tempted by the cheaper cost of 'short' certifi-cates – they contain an incomplete extract of the full entry in the register, and are of no use to family historians.

Civil registration was set up only gradually throughout the UK, starting on 1 July 1837. It was first established on the following dates:

| | |
|---|---|
| England and Wales | 1837 |
| Irish non-Catholic marriages | 1845 |
| Scotland | 1855 |
| Ireland | 1864 |

# ENGLAND AND WALES, FROM 1837

## Registration districts in England and Wales

You are probably well acquainted with the counties of England and Wales. However, for civil registration, each county was divided into superintendent registration districts. Within each of these were a number of smaller registration districts, each including about seven civil parishes. Small villages were incorporated into larger registration areas and large towns were divided into several registration districts. (These registration districts were later used for the organisation of the census – make a note of 'yours' now, and you may save some time when you come to look at the census.)

This can lead to confusion when you are searching the indexes, as they give the registration district as the place of the event. You may not recognise this as the place where you expected your ancestor to be. If you can, get acquainted with the geography of the area where your ancestors lived; or else take a map with you on your search. For help, consult *An Index to Civil Registration Districts of England and Wales, 1837 to date*, compiled by Newport. At the Family Records Centre you can check where the registration district was on maps (on the wall and available for sale).

## Scope of civil registration in England and Wales

District Registrars were appointed to issue certificates and to record births and deaths in books of prescribed stationery. Their duty was to collect information rather than passively receive it, and they were paid according to their success in making the register as complete as possible. The registrars also performed civil marriage ceremonies at their offices and supervised and recorded the weddings of nonconformists.

The parish clergy created marriage records for Anglicans, as marriage was one of the sacraments. Two registers were completed, one for the Church and one for the state. In 1898 the rules were relaxed somewhat for nonconformists, allowing other authorised persons to preside in religious ceremonies. Quakers and Jews kept their own records.

Certified copies of the registers were sent each quarter to the Registrar General in London. When the local registers became full, they were passed to the local Superintendent Registrar for safekeeping. From these the Superintendent had district indexes compiled. These registers and indexes are still kept locally.

At first there were no penalties for failing to register, so the records were inevitably incomplete. In 1875 penalties were introduced for parents who did not register births within 42 days, but it remained a common belief that baptism automatically registered a child. Before 1875 poor people were less likely to register their children than the better off, and children who died soon after birth were also more likely to be missed. It is probable that at least a third of the population is missing from the birth and death registers between 1837 and 1875, although the continuing church and chapel registers of baptisms and burials may still record some of these people.

## Information on birth certificates

- child's forenames
- sex
- date of birth
- place of birth
- mother's full name and maiden name
- father's full name and occupation if married to the mother (or, after 1875, if he attended with the mother and signed the registration entry)

- name, address and relationship to the child of the person who registered the birth
- from 1969 only: place of birth of both parents

## Information on marriage certificates

- date of marriage
- place of marriage
- whether by banns, licence or certificate
- name and age of bride and groom ('full age' = over 21)
- name and age of groom
- marital status of bride and groom
- current address of bride and groom
- occupations of bride and groom
- name and occupation of the fathers of bride and groom
- names of witnesses

## Information on death certificates

- full name
- date of death
- place of death
- given age (not guaranteed to be exact)
- cause(s) of death
- occupation (or name and occupation of her husband, if the deceased was a married or widowed woman)
- name, address and family relationship (if any) of the person who reported the death
- from 1969 only: date and place of birth, usual address at death, and the maiden name if a married or widowed woman

# Registration of births out of wedlock

This is a murky area. There are many certificates that are clearly for illegitimate children, as the father is not named. The child therefore has the mother's surname. Between 1837 and 1875, the mother could state the name of the father if she wished, and he would be included in the certificate. From 1875 the father had to appear at the registry himself to certify paternity, and give the child his name.

If the couple wanted to, there was nothing to stop them registering the child in the man's name, even if not married (except possibly respect for the law, or for the local knowledge of the registrar). A marriage certificate did not need to be produced to register a child. There are echoes here of a much older attitude to marriage, whereby a 'common-law marriage' was recognised by the community even if not by the church or by the General Register Office.

Under the Legitimacy Act 1926 it became possible in the eyes of the law for children to take their father's name after registration if he married the mother. This was done by a second registration that would have to be searched for separately.

ⓘ **Remember**

- Divorce was very rare until the 1920s, and not common till the late 1940s. Common-law marriages were probably more usual than we now recognise.

- People who had families with a new partner, after separating from their spouses, had to wait until their first spouse died to remarry legally and thus to legitimise their children. In these cases the children might only take their father's surname when their parents married.

- A way round this, to avoid the public consequences, was for the mother to change her surname to that of the father, so that any children also had the same name and thus appeared legitimate. Changes of name for this purpose are very difficult to find, as it could be done quietly (and quite legally), or even casually: if people did this, they are unlikely to leave an obvious paper trail behind them.

## Records of adoptions

Records of adoption were not begun until 1927. Before that it can be very difficult to trace the births of adopted children, since knowledge of their surnames at birth will most likely have been lost. In the past most adoptions have been purely private arrangements.

Indexes to the registers of adoptions compiled since 1927 are held at the FRC. Adoption certificates, which replace the original birth certificate for official purposes, include the following information:

- date of adoption
- name of child being adopted
- names and addresses of the adoptive parents

Access to the original birth certificate is restricted to the adopted person only. You need to contact the ONS for more advice on this. They produce a leaflet, and their website (http://ons.gov.uk/) gives more details.

## WHERE TO FIND CERTIFICATES OF BIRTHS, MARRIAGES AND DEATHS

Local registrars sent in quarterly returns to the Registrar General, but also kept their own local registers. As a result, there are two series of registers, equally valid. The best known is the central one, with its composite index, covering England and Wales. However, there are also the local ones, with their own indexes, which cover the local Registration District only. You can get copies from either, although the index references obviously won't be inter-changeable.

# Local registers

If you find that your family has not moved much, you may find that the local registers are easier to consult than the central one.

You should also find that the local indexes are more accurate than the central one. The central index was created from copies of copies, and therefore contains more mistakes. It may be worth checking with the relevant local office if you can't find an entry you are looking for in the index to the central register.

Local civil registers are normally still kept by the local registry offices: the best way to find out where they are is to check a website on the internet which acts as a reference library for family historians. This is the GENUKI website: http://www.genuki.org.uk/ There you will find a list of registration districts, by county, with the address where the local registers are kept, and advice on how to contact them, whether you can make an appointment to search the local indexes, and how to order copies. (If you don't have access to the internet yourself, ask at your local library, or try the telephone directory for the registry office.) Remember, though, that aiding family historians is not the main function of the registry offices, and don't overburden them.

# The central registers

The central civil registers are not available for the public to consult in person. You have to order and pay for copies of individual entries in the registers, which come in the form of certificates. If you supply precise references, the copy is cheaper. A fee is charged for each copy, whether it is the right one or not. Remember not to go for the cheaper 'short' certificates, as these don't include all the information in the register.

The precise references can be found by looking at the indexes to the central register. These indexes list the events alphabetically by name in the year (or quarter) in which they were registered, giving the registration district, the volume number of the register and the page number in the volume.

There are various places where you can search the indexes to the central register of births, marriages and deaths records. The main place for England and Wales is the Family Records Centre, but many local libraries and archives can also give you access to the central indexes on microfiche or microfilm, although their holdings of the indexes may not be complete. Check out the holdings of your county or borough library on the website http:www.earl.org.uk/familia/ – remember, the indexes referred to there are copies of the central indexes, not of the local ones.

Once you have found the references, you can order a copy by post, phone or internet from the General Register Office of England and Wales, at the address given on p. 17.

## Family Records Centre

The best resource for researching birth, marriage and death records for the *whole* of England and Wales is the Family Records Centre (see pp. 14–16 for details). On the ground floor are held the indexes to all births, marriages and deaths entered in the central register in England and Wales since 1 July 1837.

The indexes are colour coded using red for births, green for marriages and black for deaths. The books are large and heavy, and a microfiche set of indexes is available for those who cannot manage the volumes.

Entries in the books are listed alphabetically by surname and then forename. Babies whose parents had not decided on a name at registration appear at the end of the relevant surname listing. The indexes record the registration district rather than the name of the place where the event occurred. Each year (until 1984) is divided into quarters as follows:

March quarter          January, February and March
June quarter           April, May and June
September quarter      July, August and September
December quarter       October, November and December

Remember that births and deaths are often registered a little while after the event, so a birth on 19 March might appear in the June index, for instance.

From 1984, the index covers the whole year.

If you find a list of people in the indexes all with the same name, the first thing to do is check the registration districts. Anyone living far away from the rest of the family is unlikely to be your relative. If the difficulty cannot be resolved in this way, the FRC will do a reference check for you for a fee. Forms are available at the information desk for you to fill in.Ask the staff for advice on completing the form.

When you have found the index reference for a certificate, you can order and pay for a copy using forms available at the information desk. Copies are available for collection after four working days or they can be sent to you by post. Remember, you can order certificates by post, fax, telephone or e-mail, direct from the General Register Office at Southport (see p. 17).

## Can't find an entry in the indexes?

Failure to find a birth, marriage or death entry in the indexes may be for these reasons:

- Before 1875 there was no penalty for non-registration and there may be omissions in the birth and death registers. You may need to look at parish and non-parochial registers until 1875. See pp. 35–57.

- Before 1927 there was no formal adoption procedure and there is no record of the birth of the adopted child under the name by which he or she was known.

- There may have been a clerical error when the entry in the local register was transferred to the central register.

- Some people were known by a forename that was not the first forename on their birth certificate.

- The child may not have been named by the date of registration. Entries under the sex of the infant are given at the end of each surname section.

- In the nineteenth century at least 10% of marriages took place after the birth of the first child.

- A birth or marriage may have been registered by the Army: see p. 58–9.

- Did the event happen somewhere outside England and Wales? Try the registers of births, marriages and deaths at sea or overseas for people normally resident in England and Wales.

People normally resident in Scotland, Ireland and Northern Ireland will be found in the registers kept there (including registers of births, marriages and deaths at sea or overseas).

# GENERAL REGISTER OFFICE FOR SCOTLAND

The best resource for researching Scottish ancestors is the archive kept in Edinburgh at the General Register Office for Scotland (see p. 18). This resource can be accessed via the internet for a fee, and at the FRC you can use Scottish Link to do this. This involves booking a computer for up to two hours at a time to search the main sources for Scottish ancestors online, and order copies of birth, marriage and death certificates. A fee is charged to use this online service and it is advisable to book time in advance. Telephone 020 7533 6438 to make a booking. The records held in Edinburgh relating to births, marriages and deaths, and available on the internet and via Scottish Link, include:

*   births, marriages and deaths in Scotland since 1855
*   legal adoptions since 1930
*   divorces since 1984
*   parish registers 1553–1854
*   censuses (1881 and 1891)

# GENERAL REGISTER OFFICES OF IRELAND AND NORTHERN IRELAND

Information on births, marriages and deaths for the whole of Ireland can be found at the General Register Office of Ireland (see p. 17). Holdings include records of:

- births, marriages and deaths for the whole of Ireland 1864–1921 and for the Republic of Ireland since 1864
- non-Roman Catholic marriages since 1845

Separate records for Northern Ireland were begun on 1 January 1922 and can be consulted at the General Register Office (Northern Ireland) (see p. 17).

A computerised index to births in Northern Ireland from 1922–93 inclusive is available in the Scottish Link area at the FRC. Access is free and it can be booked in half-hour blocks on a first come, first served basis.

# BEFORE 1837:
# RELIGIOUS REGISTRATION OF
# BIRTHS, MARRIAGES AND DEATHS

## What happened before civil registration?

Civil registration was set up to provide a system covering all inhabitants of England and Wales, no matter what their religion. Before 1 July 1837 no national records were kept. An attempt had been made in 1538 to set up such a national system when the Church of England was required to keep parish registers of baptisms, marriages and burials. After 1538, religious diversity developed rapidly, and so the parish registers no longer covered everything.

The parish registers covered most people, as the Anglican Church remained the majority church. They are still kept locally, usually by county or diocesan record offices, sometimes by the parish church itself. Only birth certificates issued by the parish authorities were accepted as evidence by the courts or by the government (officers in the Army and Navy, for example, had to produce certificates from the parish records).

However, about a quarter of the population, by the late 18th century, were not Anglicans but Protestant or Catholic nonconformists. There were several unsuccessful attempts by nonconformists to make their registers, and certificates from them, acceptable as legal proof. As part of the introduction of civil registration, the nonconformists finally won the argument over the acceptability of their old registers. The General Register Office collected most of the old nonconformist registers in 1837, and checked them for accuracy. After they had been approved, the Registrar General was prepared to issue certificates from them, as from the civil registers. Another collection was made in 1858. In 1961, however, they were transferred to the Public Record Office, and they can now be freely seen either there or at the FRC. Registers not collected then are now in local record offices.

Religious registration by both Anglicans and nonconformists continued (and continues still) after the introduction of civil registration in 1837. Both types of register tend to be deposited in local record offices.

## Anglican register or nonconformist register: where to look first

Unless there is a strong probability that a family was settled in a particular parish, a good place to start is with a summary of material from Anglican parish and non-conformist registers, made by the Church of Jesus Christ of Latter-day Saints. You may find this in different formats, as technology advances. It is usually known as the *International Genealogical Index (IGI)*, on microfiche. This covers the whole world: obviously you need to search only the relevant country! The *IGI* indexes births, baptisms and marriages, but not deaths. Very usefully, it gives the name of the Anglican parish or nonconformist chapel where the event took place. This affects where you look for the actual document, as parish and nonconformist registers have ended up in different places.

The *IGI* contains huge numbers of records but the information given is not complete and therefore needs to be checked. The *IGI* can be searched at the FRC, the PRO at Kew, the Guildhall Library in London, the Library of the

Society of Genealogists in London (for a fee), and more locally through the Family History Centres of the Church of Jesus Christ of Latter-day Saints; see also *Familia* (http:www.earl.org.uk/familia/) for holdings of the *IGI* by county and borough libraries. It has been supplemented recently by the *British Isles Vital Records Index*, on CD-ROM, which can be seen at the FRC and other places.

The *IGI* is also included in a computer compilation called *FamilySearch*. This contains millions of facts relevant to family historians. They are collected from a variety of sources, ranging from the *IGI* to information given by individuals researching their own family histories. Its greatest value is for records before 1837. It is a wonderful resource, and highly addictive – but you do need to know at least basic information before you can identify *your* family members from it.

*FamilySearch* on CD-ROM can be accessed at LDS Family History Centres, at the FRC, at the PRO in Kew, and at a number of libraries throughout the UK and overseas. It is also available on the internet (http://www.familysearch.org/). To get the best out of it, it would be worth investing in the little booklet by Hawgood, *FamilySearch on the Internet*.

## Where to find Anglican parish registers

Many parish records are still kept locally, though they have usually been transferred to the nearest record office. You can find local record offices (usually the County Record Office) in the telephone directory, or through the inexpensive booklet by Gibson and Peskett, *Record Offices and How to Find Them*. Always telephone before you visit to check that they hold the register you require. You may need to book an appointment, too.

The registers of Anglican churches which were not part of the parish system are now mostly in the Public Record Office: see p. 43.

There are some further major sources of information on parish registers:

- You can find out where a particular register for England, Scotland or Wales is now kept in *The Phillimore Atlas and Index of Parish Registers* edited by Humphery-Smith. (This also indicates if there are any non-conformist records for that place in the PRO.)

- The Society of Genealogists has an extensive library, which includes a collection of over 9,000 transcripts of parish registers, listed by county.

- Scottish registers are largely included on the computer index mentioned above on pp. 34, which can be accessed at the FRC and on the internet.

Unfortunately many of the Irish registers were destroyed by fire in 1922. Those that remain are largely held in the Irish National Archives.

## Where to find nonconformist registers

All those nonconformist registers (mostly Protestant, but some Catholic) gathered by the General Register Office are now held by the PRO and can be searched either at the FRC or at the PRO in Kew. Others are held by local record offices (who have often bought microfilms of the PRO holdings for their area as well), or by the existing congregation. Most Jewish communities refused to give up their registers, and still hold them. Jewish records have often been deposited at synagogues, Jewish institutions or Jewish burial societies and cemeteries. Others have since been deposited at local record offices. The whereabouts of Protestant, Catholic and Jewish records can be found in the *National Index of Parish Registers*.

For more information on nonconformist registers, see the fuller section on pp. 52–5.

## PARISH REGISTERS

Parish registers were begun in England and Wales in 1538, in Scotland in 1552 and in Ireland in 1634. They do not survive as early as that for most parishes, and it has been estimated that the average start date of surviving registers is 1611 for England, 1708 for Wales, a little later for Scotland and the late 18th century for Ireland. Very few survive for Ireland.

Parish registers were the responsibility of the local clergy, and were kept at the church. While there were official register books, there was no uniform style imposed for keeping them so that the style and content is variable, depending on the individual record keeper. When searching for your ancestors in parish registers, you need to bear in mind the following points:

- In some parish registers records of births, marriages and deaths were intermingled and recorded as they happened. In others they were separated – sometimes in three columns on the same page, and sometimes by dividing the book into three sections.

- Since the books were expensive, it was common practice to go back through a book once it was finished and fill in any blank space, thus confusing the order of the records.

- Spelling was at the discretion of whoever was completing the records. Try saying the name out loud – it has probably been spelled phonetically.

- There is a big gap in the keeping of parish registers in 1642–60, caused by the civil war. Some of the records that do survive from this period have clearly been completed much later, probably from memory.

- Before 1733, when English became the officially designated language for legal documents, it was common to use Latin in the parish registers.

# Bishops' transcripts of parish registers

From 1597 the churchwardens of each parish in England and Wales were required to make a copy of the parish register every year, and to send it in to the bishop. The copies are usually known as the bishops' transcripts, although sometimes they are referred to as archdeacons' transcripts, or even just parish register transcripts. There are no transcripts for the period 1642–60. Transcripts made after 1754 tend to be more complete than those made before. After 1837, the making of transcripts stopped, either immediately or over the next few years.

The transcripts are obviously of most use where the original parish register cannot be found. However, the copying was not always done accurately, especially when it came to spelling. Although it's a good idea to look at the bishop's transcript if it exists, you may find that it doesn't contain exactly the same information as the original register.

These transcripts are usually, but not always, held in local record offices. For more information, see Gibson, *Bishops' Transcripts and Marriage Licences.*

---

ⓘ **Remember**

Where both a parish register and its transcript have survived, discrepancies between the two will appear as separate entries in the indexes to the records.

---

## Non-parochial Anglican records

Not all Anglican churches were parish churches, yet many of these also kept registers of baptisms, marriages and burials in exactly the same way as parish registers. They were handed in to the General Register Office when it was established, and most later went to the PRO. The main collections are:

- registers kept by the armed forces (see p. 58–9)
- Chelsea and Greenwich military and naval hospitals
- Sheerness Dockyard Church
- prisons
- chapels royal at St James' Palace, Whitehall and Windsor Castle
- Mercer's Hall, Cheapside, London
- British Lying-in Hospital at Holborn, London

The general advice given for searching parish registers also applies to these oddments.

## Searching for baptismal records in parish registers

In 1812 a standard form was introduced for the recording of baptisms that required the following information:

- date when the baptism took place (not the date of birth)
- child's Christian name
- family name

- parents' Christian names
- family address
- father's occupation
- name of the person conducting the ceremony

Before this the records tended to be less informative, though Scottish records more often noted the mother's maiden name and recorded births as well as baptisms.

The main inconvenience you are likely to come across is that the parish registers were never intended to record births, only baptisms. Moreover there has never been a legal requirement in the British Isles to have your children baptised. The following difficulties arise:

- If a person was not baptised, there is unlikely to be a surviving official record of their birth.

- Even amongst practising Anglicans a baby that was never baptised, perhaps because it died soon after birth, was not rewarded.

Women often went back to their own mothers or sought support from other members of the family or friends when they were about to give birth. Travelling a short distance might easily take them into a different parish, where the baptism might take place. Or maybe the whole family moved house between the birth dates of two children. It is always worth being aware of the surrounding parishes in your area of interest.

Some women went into lying-in hospitals to have their babies. Lying-in hospitals, such as the British Lying-in Hospital at Holborn, kept their own registers. Some of these are now held by the PRO.

---

ⓘ **Remember**

Although infant baptism was the norm, it was not unknown for people to be baptised long after they were born. For example, a nonconformist who decided to join the established Anglican church may have been baptised as an adult into that church.

---

When a baby was baptised hurriedly after birth because it was expected to die, this was sometimes registered as a 'half' baptism.

- Parents frequently waited until they had had several children before baptising them all together.

- When so many children died, it was commonplace to reuse Christian names in order to keep them in the family.

- The custom of handing down Christian names from parent to child was very strong, especially in Scotland.

- People are not always known by their baptismal name.

- Sometimes people were baptised twice, for instance to reaffirm their legitimacy so that the line of inheritance was clear.

- Sometimes the baptisms of illegitimate children were registered separately from legitimate children.

## Searching for marriages in parish registers

Traditionally weddings have taken place in the parish where either the bride or groom lived, so these are the starting point for any search of the marriage records. Sometimes marriages were registered in both the bride's and the groom's parishes. Often, however, the married couple went to live somewhere new immediately after the wedding, making marriages the most difficult to find of the three types of record covered in this Pocket Guide.

The information given in the early parish registers about couples getting married is often very brief, consisting only of the names of the bride and groom and the date. Sometimes only the groom's name is given. The Marriage Act 1753 introduced a more formal layout for marriage records, which from 1754 had to include the following information:

- date

- place (this had to be a parish church or a licensed chapel in which the banns had been called)

- whether the marriage was by banns or by licence

- that the parents had given consent if either bride or groom was younger than 21

- signatures of the minister who performed the marriage, the marrying couple, and two witnesses

The registers did not have to be written on prescribed stationery so the amount of information given continued to vary until the Marriage Act 1812 was passed to tighten up the procedure. Even then it was not obligatory to include the wife's maiden name until 1911.

The Marriage Act 1753 was also significant because it specified that a wedding was only legitimate if it was carried out in an Anglican church, either after banns had been called or a licence granted. The banns were read out in public in the parish churches of both bride and groom and they were married three weeks later. The licence was purchased in private usually from the archbishop, bishop, archdeacon or surrogate and the wedding could then take place immediately. In difficult cases the Archbishop of Canterbury might grant a special licence.

Many nonconformist chapels that had been conducting marriage services were disqualified by this Act of 1753 (with a few exceptions discussed below) so that even if you know your ancestors were nonconformists, you still need to search the parish registers for records of their marriages around this time.

In Scotland the customs surrounding marriage were different, and the Marriage Act 1753 was not enforced. In Scotland it was possible to be married by mutual consent. A good way to circumvent your parents' disapproval if you wanted to be married before you reached the age of consent in England was to go to Scotland. This applied especially if you lived in the north of England. You did not have to go to Gretna Green. The Scottish parish registers are held at the General Register Office for Scotland.

Apart from the *IGI* and its offshoots, explained on pp. 37–8, there are a number of specialist indexes covering marriage records including:

- *Boyd's Marriage Index*, organised by county

- *Pallot's Marriage Index*, which includes, amongst thousands of others, records for the City of London 1780–1837

- *Phillimore's Marriage Registers*

A full list of accessible marriage indexes is given in Gibson and Hampson, *Marriage, Census and Other Indexes for Family Historians*.

If you have no clear idea when a marriage you are looking for took place, start looking around the birth of the first child. Most frequently, marriages took place in the year before the first child was born, but quite often they also happened just after the birth.

## ⓘ Remember

- Divorce was rare, so people who took a second partner after their first marriage split up could not legally remarry unless their original spouse died.

- Widows who remarried would be more likely to do so under their married name than their maiden name.

- The age of consent has varied in England and Wales over the years. It was 21 from 1754 to 1970.

- In the 18th century boys could get married aged 14 and girls aged 12 with their parents' consent.

- People's ages recorded in parish registers are often wrong. There might be many reasons to conceal your true age, the chief one being that you were below the age of consent.

- People also tended to exaggerate their job titles to impress the in-laws or the congregation.

## Fleet marriage registers

The PRO at Kew holds a number of interesting 17th and 18th century registers kept by unbeneficed clergymen, who made a living by marrying people covertly in places that were outside the boundaries of ecclesiastical jurisdiction. The most famous of these places was Fleet Prison. Of course it was in the nature of these weddings that the participants had something to hide, so the registers cannot be taken at face value. However, there is also some evidence that many working class Londoners also regularly got married this way. These records will shortly be available at the FRC on microfilm.

## Searching for deaths in parish records

Parish registers include the following information on burials:

- date and place of death
- full name of deceased
- sex
- age (from 1866)
- occupation
- cause of death
- signature, title and address of the person registering the death
- date of registration
- registrar's signature
- the letter P in pauper burials, to show that it was at the parish's expense

From 1813, burials had to be recorded in a separate book from marriages and births and according to a stipulated format.

Scottish records include the following additional information:

- marital status of deceased
- name of spouse
- birthplace of deceased
- names and ages of children and whether alive or dead

However, Scottish registers were not usually kept as assiduously as English records, because they were the responsibility of the managers of the graveyards, rather than the clergy.

---

### ⓘ Remember

Favourite names were handed down within families, and can be confusing. It can be difficult to determine from the register whether it was the parent or the child of the same name who died at a particular time, especially soon after a birth.

---

Most people died and were buried in their local parishes, and the records can be consulted in the local record office. Some independent collections have also been made including:

- London burial records in the Guildhall Library and the London Metropolitan Archives

- York and Durham burial records, at the Universities of York and Durham

There were various reasons why someone might not be buried in the parish of their residence:

- If they died during an epidemic they might have been buried in a mass grave away from people's homes.

- If they died whilst in service it was the responsibility of the head of the household to bury them, but not to meet the expense of transporting the body any distance.

- If they died in an accident they might be buried near where it happened.

- It was common for the elderly to become destitute and have to go to the workhouse when they could no longer support themselves by working. Before 1834, many workhouses kept their own registers of deaths. Most of these registers have now been deposited at local record offices.

See pp. 56–7 for more information on cemeteries.

## NONCONFORMIST REGISTERS

A significant proportion of the population – perhaps a quarter – could not be counted as part of the Church of England. Before 1644 both Protestant and Catholic nonconformists were persecuted, and were unlikely to keep written records of their own. Even after 1644, if they wanted to ensure the legitimacy of their children they were obliged to marry in the Church of England, and quite often when they died they had to be buried in the parish churchyard. In these cases the events would either remain unregistered or appear in the ordinary parish records. This tendency was backed by force of law between 1754 and 1837, through the Marriage Act 1753. The Act recognised as legal only marriages performed by beneficed Anglican clergy. The only exceptions given were for Quakers and Jews.

Despite these various discouragements, many nonconformist congregations did establish their own registers. As there were no parishes the registers tended to be kept in the possession of individual ministers or chapels. Sometimes people would travel long distances to be baptised or married by the minister of their choice, so that these registers do not apply very strictly to any particular area.

Most Protestant nonconformist registers from before 1858 are now in the Public Record Office. Their existence is briefly indicated in *The Phillimore Atlas and Index of Parish Registers*. The registers are mostly in collections called RG 4 and RG 8. You can access the PRO catalogue on its website (http://www.pro.gov.uk/), and do a key word search using the place name. Search through first RG 4 and then RG 8, to see what survives for the locality you are interested in. It's better not to put in the denomination, as the keyword search only picks up exact matches. The PRO has a few Catholic registers: check the *National Index of Parish Registers* for others.

# Quakers

The Quakers began their own meticulous record keeping in 1613. Their registers were considered reliable enough to allow the Quakers to be exempted from the terms of the Marriage Act 1753. Quaker records have significant differences from other registers – their own dating system, for a start, and a structure based on meetings, not places. Many surviving Quaker registers and records are held at the PRO in Kew, and information from them has also been incorporated in the *IGI*. These are in the collection called RG 6. This is being filmed, and will be made available at the FRC. Another source of information on Quaker records is the Society of Friends, Friends' House Library, Euston Road, London NW1 2BJ. Copies of the Quaker registers were also made and returned to the relevant Meeting. You really need to consult Milligan and Thomas, *My Ancestors were Quakers*, to understand these records.

## Central registers of nonconformist births

Later there were two attempts to compile centralised registers for nonconformists:

- **General Register of the Births of Children of Protestant Dissenters of the Three Denominations**, founded in 1742 at Dr Williams' Library. This was a service set up to cover London and its surrounding area, but the families using it spread far further afield. The three denominations were Baptists, Independents and Presbyterians. The register's coverage eventually extended from 1716 (through retrospective registration) to 1837. About 50,000 births were registered. About 85% have now been included in the *British Isles Vital Records Index* (see p. 38).

- **Methodist Metropolitan Registry**, founded in 1818. This was a register of births and baptisms for Wesleyans throughout the British Isles. With retrospective registration its eventual coverage extended from 1773 to 1838. This register should be searched in conjunction with parish registers, as the Methodists remained within the Church of England until the 1790s.

## Nonconformist burials

Many nonconformists were buried in parish graveyards because there was no alternative. Sometimes they were buried at night so as not to attract attention. Often their burials were not entered in the register. Gradually more nonconformist cemeteries were established, usually related to individual chapels. Bunhill Fields was established in London as early as 1665. Eventually nonconformists' right to register their own communities was recognised in the Registration of Burials Act 1864, which provided for the official recording of burials at nonconformist grounds. The PRO holds many of the earlier registers of these burial grounds, among the collections of nonconformist records in RG 4 and RG 8.

# OTHER SOURCES

## Cemetery records

In the 19th century private companies began to undertake the development of a number of cemeteries around London and other large cities. For information on the London ones, see Wolfston, *Greater London Cemeteries and Crematoria*. The main cemetery records in the PRO are those of the

- Bethnal Green Protestant Dissenters' Burying Ground, (Gibraltar Burying Ground) 1793–1837 (RG 8/305–314)

- Bunhill Fields Burial Ground, City Road, London 1713–1854 (RG 4/3974–4001, 4288–4291 and 4633, with indexes in RG 4/4652–4657); other records, including an alphabetical list of persons buried 1827–1854 are kept in the Guildhall Library

- Bunhill Burial Ground or Golden Lane Cemetery, London 1833–1853 (RG 8/35–38)

- Victoria Park Cemetery, Hackney, London 1853–1876 (RG 8/42-51; each volume is arranged in letter order)

- South London Burial Ground, East Street, Walworth, London, 1819–1837 (RG 4/4362)

- Southwark New Burial Ground, London 1821–1854 (RG 8/73–74)

- Necropolis Burial Ground in Everton, Liverpool (for *all* denominations) 1825–1837 (RG 4/3121)

Monumental inscriptions from tombstones in churches and cemeteries have been transcribed by many family history societies. Try the Society of Genealogists for a central collection of these transcripts.

## Local papers

If you get totally exasperated looking for a particular record, it may be worth searching the announcement columns of the local newspaper in the town where the birth, marriage or death occurred. Archives of local papers are often found in public libraries. Check the *Familia* website (http://www.earl.org.uk/familia/), or try the British Library Newspaper Library at the following address.

▼ British Library Newspaper Library
  Colindale Avenue
  London NW9 5HE
  Telephone: 020 7412 7356

# BEFORE PARISH REGISTERS

If you are lucky enough to trace your family back to the early parish registers, you will need to develop some more skills to get back further. Not everyone, however skilful they are, can do it: the luckiest are those whose ancestors were manorial tenants *or* manorial lords! You will need some Latin and the ability to read the handwriting, but these can be learned. For help with Latin, try *Latin for Local and Family Historians*, by Stuart. There are several guides to palaeography (learning to read the writing), such as *Examples of Handwriting 1550–1650*, by Buck.

# BIRTHS, MARRIAGES AND DEATHS IN THE ARMED FORCES, FROM 1761

The ONS has a series of registers for the armed forces, which are described below. Indexes, where they exist, can be seen at the FRC and the PRO. Certificates have to be bought from the ONS, from the information given in the indexes. See p. 17 for buying copies.

## Births and marriages; and deaths outside the main wars

From 1761 to 1924, regiments in the Army kept their own registers of births and marriages, at home and abroad. The births are indexed, but the marriages aren't. You have to ask at the FRC (or direct to the ONS) for a marriage search, giving the husband's regiment and the approximate date.

There is an overlapping series of Army chaplains' returns of births, marriages and deaths, for soldiers serving abroad 1796–1880. These are indexed.

From 1880, there are returns of births, marriages and deaths abroad for the Army and Navy, joined in 1920 by the RAF. These are indexed. From 1966 they are in the general registers for events abroad.

## Deaths in the Boer War, and the World Wars

The ONS at the FRC holds the following indexes to war deaths:

- Natal and South Africa Forces, Boer War 1899–1902

- First World War deaths including the Army, RAF, Navy and the Indian Services 1914–21

- Second World War deaths including the Army, RAF, Navy and the Indian Services 1939–48

Certificates issued by French and Belgian authorities of deaths of British servicemen in hospital, 1914–1920, are at the PRO.

The Commonwealth War Graves Commission was set up to commemorate the dead of the First World War and has done its best to find and record as many war deaths as possible, from both the First and Second World Wars. Contact the Commonwealth War Graves Commission, Information Office, 2 Marlow Road, Maidenhead, Berkshire SL6 7DX, telephone 01628 34221 or visit their website at http://www.cwgc.org/

# BIRTHS, MARRIAGES AND DEATHS
## AT SEA, FROM 1851

The civil registration of births, marriages and deaths at
sea was made the responsibility of the Registrar General
of Shipping and Seamen (RGSS) in 1851. Returns were
made to the RGSS, and entered into registers, which are
now held by the PRO. However, the RGSS then made further returns from their registers to the General Register
Offices of England and Wales (now the ONS), Scotland,
Ireland and Northern Ireland of events relating to British
citizens only.

You can therefore either look at the RGSS indexes and
registers at the PRO (which include people who were not
British citizens), or buy certificates after looking at the
indexes kept by the General Register Offices in the usual
way (see pp. 16–18).

# BIRTHS, MARRIAGES AND DEATHS
## OF BRITONS ABROAD

There is no centralised collection of records of births,
marriages and deaths of Britons abroad. The ONS holds
a large collection of these records, largely relating to
English and Welsh citizens in countries that were not
colonies. The Scottish and Irish General Register Offices
also have similar registers relating to the Scottish and

Irish. The PRO also holds records relating to births, marriages and deaths of Britons abroad 1627–1965, mostly in foreign countries, but some from colonies. The Guildhall Library in London is another place to check, and so is the British Library.

## Colonial records of births, marriages and deaths

The British colonies set up and retain their own registers. These have to be searched in their country of origin, though the Society of Genealogists holds microfiche copies of, and indexes to, the Australian registers 1790–1900. The most complete set of colonial records accessible in the UK is those of British citizens (and Europeans) in India 1698–1948, with some records covering 1948–52 and up to 1968. These are held with the records of the India Office at the British Library, 96 Euston Road, London NW1 2DP.

Miscellaneous records, mostly of religious registers that were sent back from the colonies to England, can be found in collections at the Guildhall Library and the PRO at Kew.

## Records of events in foreign countries

Civil registration of English and Welsh in foreign countries began in 1849, of Scots in 1860 and of Irish in 1864. The indexes of the ONS, for English and Welsh people registered before British consuls abroad, can be searched at both the FRC and the PRO. The Scottish and Irish indexes are in the General Register Offices of Scotland, Ireland and Northern Ireland.

The registers were kept in the care of the local embassies and consulates until they were full, when they were returned to the home country. Returns had to be made regularly to the General Register Offices. There are therefore several sets of records available in the UK:

- the registers compiled from the consular returns by each of the General Register Offices

- the consular registers for each consulate, from which the returns were made (at the PRO)

- an overlapping set of religious registers, predating and continuing with civil registration (at the PRO and the Guildhall Library)

Only the last two types can be freely seen: with the registers kept by the General Register Offices, you have to buy certificates in the same way as for events in the United Kingdom.

There is no single best guide to what exists where. You need a combination of Yeo, *The British Overseas*, and chapter 4 of Bevan, *Tracing Your Ancestors in the Public Record Office*, to see the range of surviving material. Bevan cross-refers to Yeo, and is probably the best place to start.

# CONCLUSION

This Pocket Guide has aimed to provide an introduction to the various sources available to the would-be family historian. It provides you with the tools and information you need to begin discovering your ancestors so that you can start to construct a family tree. Family history is an absorbing and exciting hobby and you may find that now you've got started you are keen to explore other records, in an attempt to add more leaves to the branches of your tree. A list of Further Reading is provided below, and we hope that this Pocket Guide has inspired you to find out more!

# FURTHER READING

A. Bevan, *Tracing Your Ancestors in the Public Record Office* 5th ed. (PRO, 1999)

W.S.B. Buck, *Examples of Handwriting 1550–1650* (SOG, 1996)

T.V. FitzHugh and S.B. Lumas, *The Dictionary of Genealogy* (1985)

J.S.W. Gibson, *Local Newspapers 1750–1920* (FFHS, 1987)

J.S.W. Gibson, *Bishops' Transcripts and Marriage Licences* (FFHS, 1991)

J. Gibson and E. Hampson, *Marriage, Census and Other Indexes for Family Historians* (FFHS, 1988)

J.S.W. Gibson and P. Peskett, *Record Offices: How to Find Them* (FFHS, 1998)

D. Hawgood, *FamilySearch on the Internet* (FFHS, 1999)

C.R. Humphery-Smith, *The Phillimore Atlas and Index of Parish Registers* (Chichester, 1984)

E. McLaughlin, *Simple Latin for Family Historians* (FFHS, 1991)

E.H. Milligan and M.J. Thomas, *My Ancestors were Quakers* (SOG, 1983)

*National Index of Parish Registers* (SOG, 1968 to present)

J.A. Newport, *An Index to Civil Registration Districts of England and Wales, 1837 to date* (1989)

D. Stuart, *Latin for Local and Family Historians: A Beginner's Guide* (London, 1995)

P.S. Wolfston, *Greater London Cemeteries and Crematoria* (SOG, 1998)

G. Yeo, *The British Overseas* (Guildhall Library, 1994)